The Shift

The Revolution in Human Consciousness

Owen Waters

Infinite Being Publishing LLC
Delaware, USA
www.InfiniteBeingPublishing.com

Printed in the United States of America.
First Printing.

Library of Congress
Control Number: 2005907940

ISBN 1-932336-22-2

Contents

The Shift

8

Part I

The Shift Unfolds

The Shift

10

The Shift to the New Reality

The Shift is the mass awakening of humanity's heart. This transformation of consciousness, the greatest one ever recorded, first became apparent in the mid-1960s and has been building momentum ever since.

The Shift is a collective transformation consisting of the sum of each individual's step forward into the New Reality. Each person, in their own time, is moving forward into a new stage of consciousness, one which brings a wider vista and an awareness that springs from the heart.

In the early 1960s, just one in fifty adults had reached this new awareness. Today, according to extensive surveys, more than one in four adults in the United States and Europe have moved into the heart space which forms the nucleus of The Shift.

The New Reality is not something vague. It is as real as the notes on a piano keyboard. It has a specific frequency, as this book will reveal. Each stage of human consciousness resonates to a specific note within the musical octave. This new stage of consciousness resonates to the note F sharp. When a person's consciousness reaches a frequency that resonates with F sharp, then - and not before then - they discover unconditional love and the ability to envision a future filled with hope and peace.

The New Reality is about discovering your true potential, about living your highest joy and serving others in the way that best fulfils your highest purpose. It's about cooperation instead of competition. It's about becoming a whole person in mind, body and spirit.

The Shift to the New Reality brings to each individual a sense of greater freedom, greater joy and personal fulfillment.

The Shift to the New Reality is all about heart-powered consciousness.

Are You A Cultural Creative?

Over fifty million Americans fit the definition of a newly emerging type of humanity, a culture that hardly existed prior to the 1960s.

In a 1990s study of more than 100,000 adults in the United States, Paul Ray and Sherry Anderson reveal that a huge 26 percent of these adults have made a comprehensive shift in their worldview, values and way of life.

In Europe, the story is very much the same. A 1997 survey conducted in fifteen European countries shows figures that are very similar to the United States.

In their book, *'The Cultural Creatives,'* Ray and Anderson summarize the typical values of this new, leading-edge group of people that they call Cultural Creatives. The Cultural Creatives are people who love nature, respect the Earth and are deeply concerned about the environment. They like to develop close relationships with each other, and to help and encourage other people to develop their abilities. They care about personal and spiritual development, and want more equality for women and all cultural groups.

Cultural Creatives would like to develop a new way of life. They are cynical of media-fed information, and want to find a new political philosophy that works in today's reality. They are not materialistically driven, and typically have their finances and spending under control. They like traveling to other countries to get to know new cultures and they want to develop a sense of community where they live. Authenticity is important to Cultural Creatives - their actions have to be consistent with their words and inner beliefs.

This means that if you are searching for better quality of life, less stress, better health, and a simpler lifestyle that includes more spirituality, then you are one of a growing number of people who have already become a part of the greatest social transformation of all time.

Historical Perspective

In the early 1960s, there were too few Cultural Creatives to appear as a distinct group in popular surveys. At that time, American culture was split evenly between two cultural groups - the Moderns and the Traditionals. Moderns reflect an ethic which actually goes back as far as the Renaissance, when European Protestantism freed the population to pursue a self-empowered work ethic rather than continuing to give their power, freedom and sense of initiative away to authority figures.

The ethic of Modernism is that newer, bigger and faster is better. Time is money, they believe, and people with more knowledge and wealth are perceived as having higher status. Almost half of American adults today are Moderns. Their self-empowered principles over the centuries have brought progress to civil freedoms, democracy, justice and equality. Moderns tend to believe that their way is the only way, and they tend to reject the values of other groups as being incorrect.

The positive contributions of Moderns to society can be appreciated when you consider the quality of life which existed before the Renaissance. At birth, in those days, your fate was sealed. You were born into a certain social, ethnic and racial group at a certain location. You were never likely to travel more than 50 miles from your birthplace during your lifetime. What work you could perform, and whom you would marry, were predetermined. You would be compelled to believe certain doctrines, as dictated by rulers, priests and elders.

Traditionals belong to a culture which, historically, reacts against the changes brought about by Moderns. They wish for a return to an older, simpler time, and they oppose modern trends such as equality for women. They believe that patriarchs should again dominate family life, that all men should be proud to

15

serve in the military, and that their moral values should be forced upon others. In post-World War II America, Traditionals formed half of the adult population. Today they number less than one-fourth of the adult population. Many have passed away, while some have converted into becoming Moderns or Cultural Creatives.

Characteristics of Cultural Creatives

Within the Cultural Creatives are two distinct sub-groups: the Core group and the Green group. Almost half of the Cultural Creatives form the Core group consisting of leading-edge thinkers who focus on inner personal development. Those in the other sub-group, the Green Cultural Creatives, focus externally towards ecology and environmental issues.

The trend-setting, Core group is typically into alternative health care. They often work as health care practitioners, and most of them want to develop more inner awareness. They shun the materialism of the Moderns as well as the intolerance the Traditionals have towards other groups of people.

Cultural Creatives cross all types of demographic groupings. They can be of any adult age category, they can live anywhere, and have any spiritual or religious affiliation. The ratio of women to men is fairly equal in the Green group, while the Core group contains 67 percent women.

People with a New Age philosophy comprise less than 10 percent of Cultural Creatives. There are as many New Agers within the ranks of the Moderns as there are within the Cultural Creatives. Many New Age Moderns are men who are still chasing the boys' toys of modern technology and are still in the process of settling down to find a deeper meaning within themselves.

Compared to other groups, Cultural Creatives read more books and magazines. Half of them are regular book buyers. They watch less television and are particularly unhappy with the quality of television news. They support, and become involved in, the arts. They like well-made, durable products, natural food, personal growth and alternative health care. They have a holistic attitude, believing that body, mind and spirit should work together. Their homes are often buffered for privacy by old-growth trees and large shrubs. Inside, these homes are typically decorated by craft pieces, books and original art pieces which have special meaning to them.

The vast majority of Cultural Creatives want a caring quality in their relationships, and they believe that every person has a unique gift to offer the world. They want to help other people, and they believe that society should have a lot more respect and reverence for nature. They want to find their purpose in life and make a contribution to society. Most of them believe that a divine nature completely permeates throughout the world. They also generally believe that people have some sort of psychic ability, such as precognition or an awareness of spirit guides.

Cultural Creatives are silent trailblazers. Most of them have no idea that there are millions of people just like them with the same values and lifestyle. When they discover that more than 25 percent of the adult population share their values, they are truly shocked and surprised.

They are a newly emerging type of humanity. They hold the seeds of a new, sustainable culture, a culture where 'quality of life' replaces 'standard of living.' Imagine how transformative their effect on society will be when they evolve into networking, voicing their values and forming representative movements.

A Society Poised at the Tipping Point

Cultural Creatives have grown enormously as a social group in recent decades. In the early 1960s, they represented an estimated 2% of the U.S. adult population. By the mid-1990s, 26% of the U.S. adult population - 50 million people - had shifted to a new worldview.

Author Paul Ray sees society today as facing a 'tipping point,' where the old culture is ending and society is poised to tip over into its new form. He says that through getting in touch with our inner selves, we will regain our passion for life and unclutter from the trappings and diversions of the old reality. He sees society finding a way past the overwhelming spiritual and psychological emptiness of the old reality.

It is obvious that we are in the midst of truly momentous changes. A massive cultural shift is in progress, and a dawning new reality is taking shape in the minds of possibility thinkers everywhere.

The Shift

The Dawning of the New Reality

The Shift into the New Reality is a consciousness revolution. It dwarfs all previous and current revolutions, including the Industrial Revolution, which swept through Britain in the eighteenth century bringing massive social and technological changes. Today's information revolution, made possible by computers and telecommunications, is transforming the face of society at an even more dizzying rate.

However, these changes pale in significance when compared with the consciousness revolution, which is transforming our very perception of the nature of the universe.

Identifying Trends In Thought

A keenly insightful social scientist, Clare W. Graves (1914-86), identified the historical phases of social progress within civilization. He came to the realization that, today, mankind is preparing for a momentous leap. This leap, he said, would be a megachange within society which would dwarf all previous changes.

21

Clare Graves was a professor of psychology at Union College, New York. In the chaotic years after World War II, he wanted to determine exactly what lies beneath human nature. Rather than comparing the conflicting theories of the day, he decided to unceremoniously dump them all! Then, he decided to figure out for himself what was happening. Graves, unfortunately, passed away in 1986, just before releasing a book which would have expanded greatly upon his life's work.

Two of his students, Don Beck and Christopher Cowan, stepped in to fill the void caused by his departure. They assembled and published the essence of his research in their book, *Spiral Dynamics*. In it, Beck and Cowan have taken Graves' theory even further, enhancing his findings by drawing from the science of Memetics, the study of memes. Memes are the social equivalent of genes, cultural units of information which self-replicate from mind to mind on a vast scale, appearing within society as new trends of thought.

Each meme starts with a few social pioneers and gradually spreads to more and more people. Eventually, critical mass is reached and the whole of society in that region makes the shift to the new meme, to the new viewpoint of reality.

So far, eight different memes have been identified and analyzed as stages in the development of society throughout recorded history. The authors of *Spiral Dynamics* refer to them using color codes. These memes, which reflect the advancement of society from its primitive beginnings up to the present, are defined by the following attributes.

Spiral Dynamics Colors and Keywords

Meme colors	Keywords	Attributes
1. Beige	Survival	Basic, personal survival.
2. Purple	Safety	Clans.
3. Red	Power	Courage, survival of the fittest.
4. Blue	Truth	Finding order and purpose in life.
5.Orange	Prosperity	Achievement, striving to succeed.
6. Green	Communitarian	Community and caring.
7. Yellow	Systemic	Responsible freedom.
8. Turquoise	Holistic	Intuitive development and global view.
9. Coral	? (undefined)	A new meme which has been identified, but not yet defined.

For our purposes, it is better to refer to memes by number only, and not by color. This will simplify their comparison with other numbered phenomena later in this book.

The Historical Development of Memes

The development of human culture throughout the ages can be seen as a progression through the stages of memes, beginning with the most basic.

Meme 1. Basic, personal survival.

This meme addresses the most primitive motivation of just staying alive.

Meme 2. Clans.

This meme is about tribal and family bonding along with superstition-filled attempts to understand the powers of nature which threaten to overpower them.

Meme 3. Courage, survival of the fittest.

This meme is about mastering the environment, fighting to break free of constraints, and sensing many gods, all of which are models of power. This is where individuals first find their personal power but, seeing reality through a worldview of separation and limited resources, compete against each other in attempts to gain advantage. As a meme which is short on thought and long on passion, societies in this stage quickly fragment into territorial, feudal-type communities surrounded by competing, enemy communities.

Meme 4. Finding order and purpose in life.

This meme is about obeying authority, regulations and externally imposed rules of behavior and morality. This meme is home to the Traditionals cultural group. It is about sacrificing the self to a greater cause for a deferred reward and dedicating allegiance to one supreme God. This social meme started to spread within civilization 5,000 years ago. Eventually, alliances arose between large-scale feudal structures and those who wished to develop extensive religious power.

Meme 5. Achievement, striving to succeed.

This meme is about fighting to win, beating the competition and achieving independence. It is home to the Moderns cultural group. It started to spread significantly in the 1700s, and was made possible by the collapse of feudalism along with a sense of increased personal empowerment, which was a side-effect of the Protestant Reformation. It gained particular strength with the founding of the United States, whose Constitution and Bill of Rights intentionally empowered and protected individual liberty.

Meme 6. Community and caring.

This meme is about unconditional love, accepting others as they are, and seeing the value of service to others. It is the beginning of spiritual understanding, including freedom of the spirit from greed, dogma, contention and other distractions from spiritual centeredness. This meme started to spread in the mid-1800s as a caring sensitivity for others.

The Green Cultural Creatives group resonates to this meme, which is the first one to embrace an awareness of environment issues and to embrace greater issues of responsible living.

Memes one through six form the first tier of human consciousness.

The Momentous Leap into the Second Tier

Clare Graves saw the first set of six memes as a first tier of human development. He called the transition of the human race into meme number seven a momentous leap, an entry into an entirely new set of memes, a new tier of consciousness.

The Shift into the Second Tier of Consciousness

The Shift is the mass migration of humanity into the second tier of consciousness. Millions of trail blazers have already made The Shift. More follow them every day. The second tier is the New Reality. When you understand the nature of the second tier, you will understand tomorrow's world.

The first tier develops intellectual skills and emotional contrast. The second tier changes the focus of personal growth to a spiritual context, expanding the vision of what can be achieved through reaching ever greater heights of human potential.

In the second tier we become less personally identified with the thought and emotions which pass through our awareness. We see emotions more as things that hold our attention, rather than as things that identify who we are. This opens up the doorway to the enjoyment of an unconditionally accepting view of life and of other people.

With the new, second tier of consciousness comes freedom from all of the fears of the prior memes, and, finally, the freedom for human cognition to focus upon its true possibilities in the world.

Clare Graves identified and cataloged two of six memes of the second tier.

Meme 7. Responsible freedom.

This meme is about flexible flow, about adapting to a world full of change. With it come big-picture views and the discovery of self-accountable, personal freedom.

This meme first started to spread after the defeat of global fascism in World War II. While most people at that time looked forward to the renewed chance to create personal prosperity, the beat generation of the 1950s emerged with its questioning of materialistic culture. This emerging movement examined Eastern philosophies, such as Zen Buddhism, in a search for answers to the mysteries of life.

In meme number seven, people act from an inner-directed core. Values come from fundamental, natural law, meaning that human rights are perceived as fundamental due to the fact that you exist.

By nature, seventh meme thinkers are self-accountable and independent within reason. They are honest in their communications and do not spend time on the rules of formality, unless they are important to those present. Seventh meme thinkers like technology for what it can do to improve life, and they value knowledge and competency above rank or status.

They enjoy the pleasures of life, without being bound by any of them, and pursue activities that express their inner joy. External fashions and trends have no bearing upon these choices. They have emotional control, meaning that they still express emotions, but these expressions are appropriate, and not uncontrolled outbursts.

This is a powerful meme in promoting the exploration of the greater possibilities of life. It creates information networks and networks of people which easily adapt to changing needs.

Seventh meme thinkers are concerned with the endangered world environment and want to restore viability and ecological order. Their motivations includes being independent within reason, knowledgeable as much as possible, and caring for others within practical limits. They are accountable to themselves as responsible individuals, yet embrace their community of associates. Rather than striving to have things or to achieve things, they prefer to pursue personal development along a pathway that is natural to them.

They can interact with people of the first six memes and speak their psychological language. They respect others' worldviews and unique habits, customs and cultures, even if they don't necessarily agree with them.

This meme brings a high sense of self-esteem based upon information as much as emotion. It brings an enlightened self-acceptance which acknowledges and accepts their own shortcomings and faults as mere stages along the way to acquiring more skills.

Memes seven and eight are home to the leading-edge, spiritually aware Core group of Cultural Creatives.

The seventh meme is the first one in the second tier of memes. Having made the jump into the second tier, it then becomes an easy step to explore beyond meme number seven.

Meme 8. Intuitive development and global view.

This meme is about spiritual awakening, learning through simply being as well as through doing. It is about becoming conscious of the superconscious and trusting intuition.

It started to spread within the cultural and spiritual awakening of the mid-1960s. Those seekers who found this pattern of thinking launched a whole new movement of spiritual awareness. This spiritual renaissance has the potential to develop the awareness to carry humanity through The Shift and into the New Reality.

This meme has a global village outlook, and seeks projects and solutions that will work well for the whole planet. It contains the vision to bring order out of chaos.

Meme 8 is the second meme within the second tier. If you practice regular daily meditation or other spiritual practices, then you are already visiting the realm of meme 8 consciousness and beyond.

The Shift

A Meme-Related Definition of Spirituality

Basic consciousness is associated with the first tier of six memes. Its function is to provide learning from the diversity of experience in the world and to gain definition as an individual. In particular, it explores duality; the idea that opposites are separate from each other, rather than facets of an underlying whole.

The duality of good versus evil, for example, is made possible by a belief in the existence of an opposite pole to goodness and wholeness. This belief, or expectation, creates the possibility that evil can exist and manifest in a world of duality. Evil cannot be conquered via conflict, as the act of conflict only adds power to the illusion which generates its existence. It can only be resolved by adopting a consciousness of unity rather than separation. Then, lasting solutions to the illusion of duality become possible.

Spiritual consciousness is associated with the second tier of six memes. With it comes the developing awareness of the oneness of all life.

Spiritual consciousness starts with an appreciation that all people are facets of the one underlying consciousness of the universe. Along with this comes an understanding that we each have our own unique viewpoint of the universe. It is through our individual diversity that the whole consciousness of humanity gains an infinite range of experience of all facets of life.

As a person becomes more at one with all of existence, they do not lose any sense of individuality. In all of Creation, diversity is the rule. Just as each snowflake is unique, so is each person.

The Mystery Meme

The authors of *Spiral Dynamics* have identified the existence of the next, new meme. This ninth meme, which they call 'coral,' has not yet been observed in large quantities of people, so they have been unable yet to summarize its characteristics.

Before we examine how to successfully operate within the New Reality, which begins primarily with meme number seven, let's look ahead and examine what discoveries await us within the mysterious ninth meme.

Second tier memes are reminiscent of their first tier cousins. The first tier of six memes is a basic, or physically-oriented, set while the second tier is cre-atively or spiritually-oriented. The second tier, being of a higher frequency band of consciousness than the first tier, will exert considerably more influence in the world as its activation becomes more widespread. As the popular use of the second tier of memes only began in earnest in the mid-1960s, we have yet to see much of its influence manifest in the world.

Meme number seven (responsible freedom) is related to its first tier equivalent, meme number one (basic, personal survival). Meme number seven means having a viewpoint from a much wider vista of con-sciousness than meme one. It deals with flexible flow

35

and with adapting to a world full of change. Meme number seven is like learning to survive all over again, but this time through a global viewpoint. It is the starting point, and the orientation course, for the entire second tier of memes.

Meme number eight (intuitive development and global view) is the second tier version of meme number two (clans). It is related to meme number two, but comes with a viewpoint that is holistic and global. Meme number eight brings the vision to create, not a local clan, but a global village or a unified clan of humanity. Unlike the small-clan focus of meme number two, meme number eight thinkers can see that the key to unity is to embrace the unlimited diversity of humanity as a whole. Integration and peace can then be created through the existence of our common humanity, when people accept everyone else as they are, simply because they exist.

This equates to the fundamental, Creator-given right of each human being for self-determination simply because they exist. People were created to experience self-determination. Humanity was created to have an endless variety of personalities for the purpose of gaining infinite varieties of experience.

At this higher level of consciousness, it becomes obvious that any attempt to coerce people into conformity with the standards of another person, or another group of people, is actually a violation against the will of the Creator.

Paradoxically, acceptance of human diversity is the key to the unity of humanity.

The Nature of the Mystery Meme

The new meme - number nine - will be like meme number three (courage, survival of the fittest), only in a higher form of manifestation. Meme number three's courage brought about adventure, exploration and mastery of the physical environment. As the second tier memes all have a creative or spiritual orientation, this means that the new meme number nine will bring about adventure, exploration and mastery of the holistic environment of mind, body and spirit. It will do this while encompassing a global scale of awareness.

The new, ninth meme will bring exploration of the spiritually-inspired use of the power of the mind to transform reality for the better. It will create a strong demand for spiritual and creative freedom on a global basis.

This far-ranging, inspiring meme has the power, quite simply, to transform the entire world as we know it.

The keywords of the ninth meme will be 'Powerful creativity.'

This is not just the type of creativity that uses the imagination to create new ideas, inventions and works of art. When this meme eventually unfolds on planet Earth, its higher form of creativity will come fully-primed with spiritual power - enough power to transform life on this planet into a whole new level of joy and harmony.

Maslow Predicted The Shift

Abraham Maslow (1908-70) was a psychologist who became famous for his hierarchy of human needs. When he developed his theory in the 1950s, he predicted the transformation of humanity into a realm of spiritual transcendence, but he had no idea just how soon this would develop into a major movement. Little did he know that, in the mid-1960s, the shift towards transcendence would suddenly take off and never look back.

Maslow's hierarchy of human needs shows that basic human needs have to be fulfilled before people can attend to higher needs and values.

First, the basic physiological needs of food and shelter must be met in order to ensure survival.

Second, once food and shelter are obtained, safety and security must be achieved.

Third, acceptance by others is sought, in both the social and romantic sense. To fulfill this 'belonging' need, people become part of a group, a tribe, an extended family or a community.

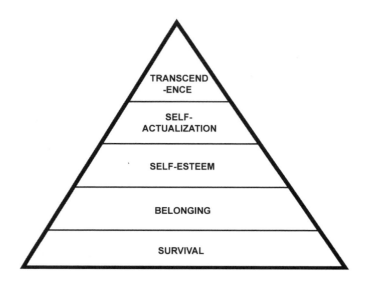

Maslow's Original Hierarchy of Human Needs

When these outer-directed needs are satisfied, then the individual works to acquire self-respect. Recognition by others produces self-esteem.

Once the outer needs are fulfilled, the inner-directed need for self-actualization comes into play. To self-actualize means to become the best you personally can be. Self-actualized people include those who have achieved material abundance, and also those who, as a decision of personal power, have chosen simplicity over the pursuit of further abundance. At some point, when a person says "That's enough" to the endless pursuit of additional financial security, then they become free to accomplish anything that inspires their inner joy the most.

Self-actualization is achieved after the individual ceases to have deference to hierarchical authority, and instead matures into the ability to make their own rules of personal responsibility. Personal responsibility is always more powerful and effective than any system of imposed rules. For example, you can threaten to punish someone if they steal and hope that the threat works. But, a self-responsible person simply doesn't steal because they wouldn't have the heart to do such a thing to another person.

It's a matter of increased maturity. When a person abandons the impositions of external authority and becomes their own, self-directed authority, then they become far more functional in the world. This is, in fact, a higher state of consciousness, one which provides a higher vista of awareness. From this expanded vista, they see clearly how they as an individual can best serve humanity.

In this state of awareness, the person acquires the ability to think and analyze situations independently. As a result, new and creative solutions spring to mind. They have enough self-esteem to be able to clearly see their own needs, skills, strengths and weaknesses, and from that they see where they can best be of service to humanity.

Once basic needs are fulfilled, the next values relate to being. The first of these being-values is self-actualization, which is the instinctual need of a human to make the most of their unique abilities.

Above that, Maslow placed transcendence, which he considered a spiritual value. Traditional universities typically presume that spiritual matters are beyond the understanding of their students, so they present the Maslow hierarchy of human needs differently. They present it with self-actualization as the ultimate human goal, and omit the transcendence stage beyond that.

The being-values of self-actualization and transcendence are the more refined and beautiful aspects of human consciousness. They include unconditional love, altruism, inner joy, a love of nature, the development of intuition (in males as well as females), idealism, and a sense of wisdom which springs from within. These skills develop the right-brain functions of creativity and intuition.

Maslow and Memes

In terms of meme equivalents, Maslow's definition of self-actualization begins with meme number 6, while his definition of the beginning of transcendence equates to meme number 7.

While people who are primarily in meme 6 consciousness are actively preparing for an imminent shift to the second tier, The Shift, as a societal movement, refers to the meme 7 stage of consciousness and beyond.

In the 1950s, Maslow believed that only 2% of the population had achieved self-actualization. The mid-1960s changed all that when masses of people began the search for the higher values, such as unconditional love and spiritual wisdom. Today, that progressive movement in society (meme 6 and above) has blossomed from 2% to over 20%, and is climbing every year. This means that more than 20% of adults have either gone through The Shift or have entered meme 6 and are, therefore, preparing for their personal shift into the second tier.

A Word About Chaos

In physics, chaos is a phase that occurs during transformation. You can resonate a container of water with sound waves that generate a balanced, symmetrical pattern on the surface of the water. Then, if you turn up the frequency a little, chaos will ensue. The neat pattern on the surface of the water will become choppy and discordant. However, when you turn the frequency up still more, a new pattern emerges, one which is even more complex and beautiful.

The chaos was a temporary phase between one natural state of harmony and its transformation into a higher form.

It is much the same with the transformation of humanity through The Shift. The frequency associated with the Old Reality has already been increased. The old pattern has been disturbed and is beginning to go away. In its place is a choppy pattern which is searching for its new form. Discords abound at a personal and social level as old wounds arise seeking attention and resolution. As the frequency rises even more, the chaotic outbreaks upon the surface of life will settle into a new pattern, one which is even more complex and beautiful.

The Cosmic Calendar

Why should society be rushing headlong into a New Reality of awareness at this particular point in history? The sudden awakening of holistic, spiritual thought in the 1960s affected the younger generation of that era. Those who were impressed and changed by, for example, the Summer of Love in the year 1967 will be at the peak of their economic and political influence by the year 2010. They will, by then, be the Elders of society, the wise ones that younger generations look to for guidance when things go wrong.

If society is ready to start moving en masse into The Shift after the year 2010, you have to wonder what cosmic events might be in synchronicity with such timing. Could there be some grand, cosmic event about to occur? How about an imminent event which occurs just once every 26,000 years? Would that pique your curiosity?

The ancient Mayan civilization existed up until 830 A.D., when they suddenly disappeared from their cities, leaving no traces behind as to where they may have moved. Despite an apparent lack of precision instruments, the astronomical knowledge of the Mayan culture exceeded today's level of knowledge in many ways. They not only knew the precise orbits of the planets in our solar system, but also the orbits of the stars in our galaxy. They had even cataloged major cosmic events going back more than 400 million years. The Mayan calendars are masterpieces which illustrate the repeating time-spirals of cosmic cycles within cycles within cycles.

The Mayans spoke of waves of influence which pass through the galaxy; waves which are so influential that they are capable of triggering the formation of suns from collections of gases. They also spoke of waves of galactic influence which have a profound effect upon human history on planet Earth.

One such critical point is a major galactic synchronization which is due to occur in the very near future, on December 21st, 2012. This date marks the end of a 26,000 year cycle of a style of human experience, as well as the end of a 5,200 year cycle within that, and also the end of many more sub-cycles, all in synchronicity with each other.

On December 21st, 2012, when the Mayan calendar again resets to zero, a new 26,000 year cycle begins. Now, 26,000-year cycles don't suddenly change from an old cycle to a new cycle in the blink of an eye. Such a huge cycle influences a period of overlap, both before and after the exact date of the change to a new cycle. The overlap period before the year 2012 would have included its early influence upon culture in the 1960s, when the current transformation in consciousness began in earnest.

The question is, when future generations look back on our current era, will they see the year 2012 as the pivotal point within The Shift? Could the year 2012 mark a turning point where the old type of humanity, Homo sapiens (*"knowing man"*), shifts into wholeness as the second tier of consciousness begins to reach popularity? Will the second tier be seen, in retrospect, as a new phase of human evolution, a kind of Homo holisticus?

One thing that is certain at this point is that The Shift is a real phenomenon and, as the Cultural Creatives and memes studies demonstrate, it is happening today. The Shift is not a temporary by-product of the baby boom generation, or of any other generation in modern society. It is not a passing fad and it is not going away.

The Shift is the result of a cosmic cycle which is unfolding and, slowly but steadily, increasing the frequency of all consciousness upon the planet.

The Shift is, to put it simply, the most wonderful transformation in recorded history. This is where humanity gets to build, literally, Heaven on Earth.

The Shift

Part II

New Discoveries

The Shift

Gateways of Consciousness in the Human Energy System

The memes observed by Clare Graves are much more than the result of a sociological study. They have their roots in the very design of the universe, in the way that human consciousness was designed to operate.

Science today, for the most part, shelters itself inside the safe harbor of materialism. However, excluding an appreciation of the works of the Creator from scientific inquiry can slow the progress of research considerably. When you base your assumptions upon the idea of the universe as an intelligent creation, then it becomes much easier to find the answers to many perplexing questions.

If humans are progressing through twelve memes of experience, then could there be a fundamental phenomenon of consciousness which supports this segmentation of consciousness into twelve distinct phases? Are memes just some odd coincidence, or are they a built-in design feature of human consciousness? As a lifelong mystic, I favor the latter, and it was this line of inquiry which led me to discover the hidden link between memes and the natural frequency bands of human consciousness.

The human energy system consists of intricate pathways of etheric, or life, energy. For our purposes, we need only refer to the major gateways where life energy, and consciousness, enter and leave the human body.

These gateways of consciousness within the human energy system are traditionally called chakras (*"shack-ras"*), meaning wheels or vortices of energy. Most reference books list seven major chakras, all of which are etherically connected to the human spine. Here is how they are typically portrayed as vortices of energy just outside of the physical body:

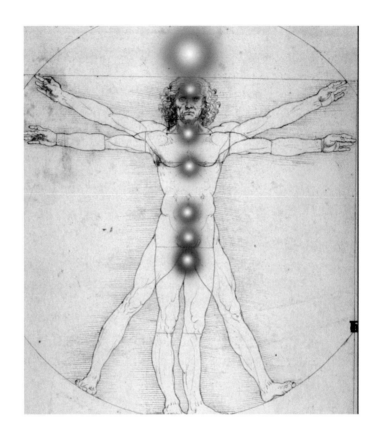

**The Seven Major
Consciousness Gateways**

The Functions of the Gateways

Using the traditional seven-chakra model, the functions of the chakras are as follows:

1. Instinctual. The root chakra prepares vitality, or life energy, for the chakras above it. It provides the base frequency of human existence including the instinct for survival.

2. Emotional. The sex chakra powers the basic emotions or passions of human life.

3. Intellectual. The solar plexus chakra is used in the development of intellect or mental ability in a linear direction. For example, arithmetic is linear, so is algebra, so are digital computer processes. Linear thinking is a logical, left-brain skill. Holistic, right-brain skills, on the other hand, include the ability to see a pattern within a whole picture.

4. Holistic. The heart chakra is developed as issues of separation become resolved and integrated. Mind, body & spirit are seen as facets of the whole human being.

5. Creative. The throat chakra's function is creativity. It is capable of inspiring the imagination to create new ideas, inventions and works of art. Its further development results in the power of conscious creation, the ability to consciously transform your

reality.

6. Spiritual. The third eye chakra is the home frequency of your soul family. While a person's closest soul mates can be usually counted on the fingers of two hands, soul families are much larger. They are extended, related groups of, typically, 2,000 individuals. When you feel a yearning for your true spiritual home, you are remembering your connection to this level of consciousness. In the cycle of reincarnation, it is to this frequency of consciousness that you ultimately ascend in spirit before planning your next physical incarnation.

7. Universal. The crown chakra is your connection to the universe on a cosmic scale. Its complete activation brings the ultimate state of human achievement and enlightenment, that of cosmic consciousness.

When Does Seven Equal Twelve?

Within the entire range of human consciousness, we have seven major chakras and twelve memes. Could there be a relationship between the two? Obviously seven does not equal twelve... unless, of course, you're playing the C octave on a piano keyboard.

There are seven white, or major, keys within each C octave, and yet an octave always contains a total count of twelve black and white keys before the sequence repeats itself in the next higher octave.

I found it eerily coincidental that there would be seven major keys within a twelve-note octave, and also seven major chakras within a frequency range covered by twelve social memes. It was as if I had stumbled upon some beautiful, synchronistic design feature within Creation, but, initially, I couldn't yet identify exactly what it was.

The Keyboard of Consciousness

Musical keyboards include several octaves. Octaves are sets of notes which run, for example, from C through D, E, F, G, A, B and up to the next C note, which also forms the start of the next octave.

A Musical Keyboard

In music, the word 'octave' literally means 'eight notes.' The C-octave is performed by playing the note C along with the next C above it, eight white keys higher. The higher C note is also the start of the next octave higher.

In the emerging science of Resonance, the view of a C-octave has to be limited to the notes within that octave – just C through B - ignoring the next C

57

note, as it actually belongs within the next octave higher.

These are the notes within one octave on a piano keyboard:

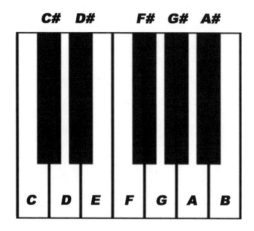

The Notes Within One Musical Octave

The sound made by Middle C on a piano keyboard resonates at 261.6 cycles per second. Each octave higher doubles the frequency. That means that the note C, one octave above Middle C, resonates at twice that rate, or 523.2 cycles per second.

Each octave on a piano keyboard contains seven major (white) keys and also five black keys.

Starting with Middle C on the keyboard, you can play just the seven white keys as you ascend towards the next octave, as follows:

Middle C, then D, E, F, G, A and B. Most of the white keys are one full tone apart from each other.

You could also play all twelve keys, both the white and the black ones, as follows:

Middle C, then C# (C sharp), D, D#, E, F, F#, G, G#, A, A# and B.

The significance of playing all twelve keys is that each one is separated from the next by exactly one half-tone, or one-twelfth of an octave. For example, D sharp is a half-tone above D and a half-tone below E.

Music and Mysticism

Most information currently published on the human chakra system indicates that the seven major chakras are related to the seven major keys on the piano keyboard. The root chakra is said to resonate to Middle C, and the resonant frequencies of the other chakras then ascend through the major keys D, E, F, G, A and B.

However, some charts of chakras are different. These claim that the solar plexus chakra resonates to the note D sharp, not E. This presents a dilemma. I could understand seven major notes resonating to the seven major chakras, but why would some people say that just one of them is a non-major key and, therefore, unlike the rest?

Symmetry is a phenomenon that supports theories in physics. Where it exists, it is said to support the theory in question. Symmetry means, basically, sameness. If you view a four-sided pyramid from any of its four base corners, it will look like exactly the same shape from each of the four viewpoints.

With piano keys, sameness would imply all white keys or all black keys. So, when you see a list of all white keys except one, then you no longer have that symmetry.

Which keys on the keyboard, I had to ask, actually matched which chakra?

I used a precision tuner, the kind that musicians use to tune their instruments, and kinesiology testing to find the answers. Kinesiology is a muscle-testing technique which reveals strength or weakness in the subtle nervous system. These strength-or-weakness conditions equate to yes-or-no answers. When your subtle nervous system registers that a chakra resonates to the musical note being played, then the test will produce a strong muscle response, i.e. a 'yes' response. Kinesiology will be described in more detail later in the chapter, 'How You Are Changing The World.'

The experiment confirmed one basic fact that everyone had said before, that the root chakra does, in fact, resonate in harmony with Middle C. Now, that does not literally mean that the root chakra resonates at the exact frequency of Middle C. It means that, in its own octave, the root chakra resonates at the note C. It resonates at a harmonic of Middle C. If you have two guitar strings tuned exactly one octave apart and you pluck one of them, then the other one will resonate in sympathy, because it is an exact harmonic. Chakras vibrate many octaves higher than the piano keyboard, and the root chakra resonates in harmony with the note C.

You can perform the exact same test yourself if you have a precision tuner, an awareness of the chakra locations, some kinesiology practice and an open mind. Kinesiology, like computer technology, operates on the GIGO principle – Garbage In, Garbage Out. If a tester has the negative mental condition of skepticism going in, then the answers coming out will also be negative. Successful kinesiology testing requires an open mind with no prior expectations.

Continuing to test the other chakras in turn, I found that the seven major chakras actually resonate, not to all seven white keys, but to the following notes:

C, C#, D#, F, G, A, B

Five white keys and… not one, but *two* black keys.

This was even worse than before! Catastrophe had struck! Now I had two odd notes out instead of just one.

So, I asked, where could the five black notes in an octave fit into a symmetrical picture alongside the seven major notes? Here we are, with twelve piano keys in an octave, but only seven chakras. How could the five center chakras all be separated from each other one full tone, while the crown and the root chakras are only separated from their neighbors by a half-tone?

This was all supposed to be so straightforward and simple. Seven major chakras, seven major keys on the keyboard. All neat and symmetrical. Except that it isn't.

When You Can't Solve a Problem, Try Turning it Around

The usual view of the major chakras is that they can all be seen from the front of the body. However, this is not entirely correct.

The crown chakra resides above the head (facing upwards), the root chakra is just below the base of the spine (facing downwards), and there are five more chakras in between.

Each of these five middle chakras has two faces - one face that looks forwards, just in front of the body, and one face that looks backwards, just behind the body.

That makes a total of one crown chakra, one root chakra and five two-facing chakras. One plus one, and fives times two, makes a total of twelve chakra *faces*.

There are twelve chakra faces within the seven-chakra system.

Symmetry had shown itself at last.

Now, if there are twelve faces in all, what if the back solar plexus chakra face is not the same as the front solar plexus chakra face? What if front and back faces of a chakra vibrate at *different* frequencies to each other? Everyone always assumed that the front face of the solar plexus was functionally the same thing as the back face. But, what if it's not?

Getting back to the twelve keyboard keys, what if they - the twelve total white keys and black keys in an octave – exactly match the twelve chakra faces?

Upon further testing, this is exactly what became apparent:

The twelve faces of the human chakra system exactly match the resonant frequencies of the twelve keys within a musical octave.

Also, a phenomenon of 'Chakra Twinning' became apparent. Chakra Twinning recognizes that, while pairs of chakra faces are related by function, they operate in a yin-yang relationship and vibrate at their own unique frequencies.

For example, the solar plexus pair of chakra faces both have an intellectual function. The front chakra face explores the passive, yin version of intellect, while the back chakra face explores the active, yang version of intellect.

New Discoveries About the Chakras

To summarize the new information which was uncovered during this research:

1. The Twelve Chakra Faces and the Musical C-Octave

The twelve faces of the chakras resonate exactly with the twelve keyboard keys within the C-octave. Each front-facing chakra face is separated from its back-facing opposite by exactly one half-tone.

2. Frequency Differences Between Chakra Faces

Each back-facing chakra resonates a half-tone higher than its front partner. The front face is therefore the lower frequency face of each chakra pair. For example, if you add one half-tone to the front face of the solar plexus chakra, you have the exact frequency of the back face of the solar plexus chakra. If you add another half-tone, you have the frequency of the front face of the heart chakra. Adding yet another half-tone, you have the frequency of the back-facing heart

65

chakra, and so on.

3. Spinal Connections

The back-facing chakras connect into the etheric equivalent of the spine approximately 1.25 inches (3 cm) above where their front-facing partners connect.

4. The Yin-Yang Relationship of Chakra Pairs

The normal flow of energy through a chakra pair is from front to back. There is a yin-yang character to the front and back faces of a chakra. The front-facing chakra is more feeling and community-oriented (yin) while the back-facing chakra is more individualistic and expressive (yang).

a) The front-facing chakras are receptive - they receive energy from the environment. For example, when you enter a room full of people, you unconsciously sense the mood within the room through the front, receptive face of your solar plexus pair of chakras.

b) The back-facing chakras are active – they transmit energy to the environment after it has been conditioned by its path through the individual. In this way, each person's thoughts and feelings contribute to the atmosphere of the global mind.

The yin-yang relationship between pairs of chakra faces is the difference between the traditional seven-chakra system view and the twelve chakra faces view. Both views are perfectly valid. However, the viewpoint of twelve chakra faces adds the idea that each of the five chakra pairs have a yin-yang relationship.

For example, the front-facing heart chakra face is the yin (predominantly receptive face) of the heart chakra pair. The back-facing heart chakra face is the yang (predominantly active face) of the heart chakra pair. As we progress in consciousness through the chakras, we first feel our way into a new chakra pair via its front face. Once we have absorbed its feeling into our emotions and our beings, then we turn to the active face of the chakra and begin to express those feelings in practical action.

This newly-recognized phenomenon of 'Chakra Twinning' recognizes that, while pairs of chakra faces are related by function, e.g. emotional-receptive and emotional-active, they differ in that they operate in a yin-yang relationship and vibrate at their own separate frequencies.

5. Chakras and Music and Memes All Match

As you are about to see, the characteristics of the known memes of Spiral Dynamics correlate exactly with the characteristics of their equivalent chakra faces. This means that three phenomena match each other in perfect symmetry:

a) The twelve faces of the chakras

b) The twelve keys of the musical octave

c) The twelve memes of Spiral Dynamics

Having two phenomena match perfectly is Symmetry. A condition of symmetry is that which supports a theory in metaphysics as well as physics.

Having three phenomena match each other perfectly is Super Symmetry. This discovery linking 1) chakras, 2) music and 3) memes qualifies as Super Symmetry. As such, it reveals a key aspect in the Creator's original design work behind the universe and human consciousness.

It also means that the memes of consciousness act in a way similar to electron orbits. When an electron has acquired sufficient energy, it suddenly makes a quantum leap to a higher energy level. When humans have acquired enough 'consciousness energy' through experience within one meme, they make a quantum leap to the next energy level and start to explore a new meme.

The Shift

Super Symmetry: Chakras, Music & Memes

The memes of Spiral Dynamics, the notes within an octave, and the system of twelve chakra faces all perfectly match one another.

The following chart data illustrates how the rise of civilization has passed through a sequence of memes which are directly related to the human chakra system.

Memes, Musical notes and Chakra locations

Meme Note		Location	Chakra function
1	C	Root chakra	Instinctual
2	C#	Sex chakra – front	Emotional-receptive
3	D	Sex chakra – back	Emotional-active
4	D#	Solar plexus – front	Intellectual-receptive
5	E	Solar plexus – back	Intellectual-active
6	F	Heart chakra – front	Holistic-receptive
7	F#	Heart chakra – back	Holistic-active
8	G	Throat chakra – front	Creative-receptive
9	G#	Throat chakra – back	Creative-active
10	A	Third eye chakra – front	Spiritual-receptive
11	A#	Third eye chakra – back	Spiritual-active
12	B	Crown chakra	Universal connection

Memes, Chakra functions and How they manifest:

Meme no.	Chakra function	Manifestation of the meme or chakra
1	Instinctual	Personal survival
2	Emotional-receptive	Clans
3	Emotional-active	Courage
4	Intellectual-receptive	Ordered purpose
5	Intellectual-active	Achievement
6	Holistic-receptive	Caring community
7	Holistic-active	Responsible freedom
8	Creative-receptive	Intuitive development
9	Creative-active	Powerful creativity
10	Spiritual-receptive	Secrets of the universe
11	Spiritual-active	Globally applied wisdom
12	Universal connection	Cosmic consciousness

This discovery of how memes correlate to natural frequency bands of consciousness allows us a larger view of the memes phenomenon. Now, we can even predict what the characteristics will be for future social memes, ones which have not yet been identified through observation.

It is now possible to map out the enormous human potential which lies ahead as each meme, on a social level, and each chakra face, on a personal level, becomes activated.

A Glimpse Into the Future

While The Shift is primarily a quantum leap into the second tier of six memes, the future will be filled with much more than just the consciousness of meme number 7. The other memes in the second tier, 8 through 12, will be beckoning to the trendsetters and pioneers in society.

Memes 8 and 9 will open up a huge wave of constructive creativity for many people. This stage of consciousness contains the vision and the ability for people to begin remaking the world as a place of deep and lasting beauty.

Constraints that we take for granted today will begin to dissolve. For example, as we discover the secrets of instantaneous travel through space, we will gain enormous freedom of movement.

Memes 10 and 11 are the memes of enlightened wisdom. Even glimpses of this rarefied level of consciousness during deep meditation allow much wisdom to flow into the awareness. The achievement of meme 12 is the ultimate, long sought-after state of cosmic consciousness, which is the true pinnacle of human potential.

As you can see, stepping forward into the second tier of consciousness opens up much more than just the next step in consciousness. It opens up a whole new stairway of exciting expansion towards the ultimate in human potential.

Next, we will look back in history to view the rise of civilization, as seen from the viewpoint of the chakras.

The Rise of Civilization

Let's now examine how civilization has worked its way through each meme so far, to see how each stage of progress has unfolded from the viewpoint of the chakras.

1. Instinctual (root) chakra: Survival

Basic survival at this level of existence is difficult at best. You're on your own, food sources are unreliable and dangers lurk in the form of large, hungry animals. Any humans who ever did live this way, quickly moved on to meme number two.

2. Emotional-receptive chakra: Clans

People realized that hanging out with each other was far less stressful than hanging out alone near large, hungry animals. This meme encouraged kinship to take front stage. Personal competition for resources took less precedence. If they could just get along, they could help protect each other.

3. Emotional-active chakra: Courage

Community is all very well, but some nagging questions eventually arose. Who's going to explore beyond the end of the world? What lies beyond those hills? Could that be the edge of the world?

Slowly, but surely, the ones with the biggest sense of curiosity ventured forth to explore the unknown. Bringing back tales of new hills and valleys full of extra food just waiting to be eaten, the younger members of the clans were inspired to become explorers too.

4. Intellectual-receptive chakra: Ordered purpose

The young and the restless gave way to the rise of natural leaders within the ranks. These new leaders reined in any wayward individuals and began to impose order by force. A creed of order was created and policed by those who, before, had been adventurers. Life was given reason and purpose. Rules were made, which were to be followed for the good of the whole. Punishments awaited those who stepped out of line.

As people settled into this meme, the foundation for the next meme and the Age of Reason was slowly being prepared.

78

5. Intellectual-active chakra: Achievement

Ordered purpose is one thing, but how long are you supposed to wait for the promised rewards? Intellectual reasoning brings with it greater vistas of possibilities than before. "Did you know," they said to each other, "that if you avoid the old tradition of becoming a monk or a soldier, then you can become a merchant and get wealthy? Then you'd be free to do what you want!"

Then, religious reform added a work ethic to the list of desirable human attributes. Now, with a moral license to be productive, individuals began to really express their potential. The spreading waves of initiative and opportunity led onwards to the Industrial Revolution, which transformed the all-pervasive, peasant class into wage-earners of comparative prosperity.

6. Holistic-receptive chakra: Caring community

We are discovering today that the problem with rampant industrial progress brings unsustainable side-effects, such as pollution through the creation and release of toxins.

When a person begins to explore the heart-centered, holistic chakra, they are likely to become environmentally aware. As more people do this, increasing pressures are applied to contain the polluting side-effects of rampant industrial growth and to introduce long-term sustainability. Polluting the planet, really, is like a teenager trashing their own room. Sooner or later, they have to grow up and become responsible for their environment. Long term, there is no other option.

This holistic-receptive chakra is where the vista of awareness expands once again and the issues that are important to a person begin to encompass the greater good of society.

7. Holistic-active chakra: Responsible freedom

This is the first stage of the second tier of consciousness. Clare Graves called this jump into the second tier of consciousness "a momentous leap" for humanity. When your primary focus becomes this holistic-active chakra, then you have personally passed through the gateway of The Shift and are functioning in the New Reality.

While the sixth chakra allowed people to acclimatize to the feel of holistic, heart-centered consciousness, the seventh chakra suddenly springs this potential into action. With this holistic-active chakra, people learn how to express that new, wide-area vision of the heart and start to make a real difference in the world.

While the sixth chakra face is heartfelt, the seventh chakra face is heart-powered.

When enough people's primary attention is focused through their holistic-active chakras, which correspond to the first meme in the second tier, then the 'hundredth monkey effect' will occur. This phenomenon was widely promoted by author Ken Keyes who said that, when it occurs, society will transform en-masse from 'you versus me' consciousness to 'you and me' consciousness. In other words, most people will suddenly appreciate the value of shifting from competition to cooperation.

The Shift

How the Hundredth Monkey Effect Works

The Hundredth Monkey Effect observes that, when a sufficiently large core group learns a new behavior, there comes a point where the new behavior spreads almost instantly to the majority of that culture.

This means that there will come a point when New Reality consciousness will suddenly make sense to the majority of people within the cultures that are currently moving through The Shift.

The Hundredth Monkey Effect was first introduced by biologist Lyall Watson in his 1980 book, 'Lifetide.' He reported that Japanese primatologists, who were studying Macaque monkeys in the wild in the 1950s, had stumbled upon a surprising phenomenon.

His book was soon followed up with a deeply inspired work by Ken Keyes in 1981, called "The Hundredth Monkey Effect." In this, Ken Keyes made an impassioned appeal for an end to the Cold War and its policy of mutually assured destruction. Here, in the words of Ken Keyes, is a description of the key elements of the Hundredth Monkey Effect:

83

"The Japanese monkey, Macaca fuscata, had been observed in the wild for a period of over 30 years.

"In 1952, on the island of Koshima, scientists were providing monkeys with sweet potatoes dropped in the sand. The monkeys liked the taste of the raw sweet potatoes, but they found the dirt unpleasant.

"An 18-month-old female named Imo found she could solve the problem by washing the potatoes in a nearby stream. She taught this trick to her mother. Her playmates also learned this new way and they taught their mothers too.

"This cultural innovation was gradually picked up by various monkeys before the eyes of the scientists.

"Between 1952 and 1958 all the young monkeys learned to wash the sandy sweet potatoes to make them more palatable.

"Only the adults who imitated their children learned this social improvement. Other adults kept eating the dirty sweet potatoes.

"Then something startling took place. In the autumn of 1958, a certain number of Koshima monkeys were washing sweet potatoes — the exact number is not known.

"Let us suppose that when the sun rose one morning there were 99 monkeys on Koshima Island who had learned to wash their sweet potatoes.

"Let's further suppose that later that morning, the hundredth monkey learned to wash potatoes.

"Then it happened!

"By that evening almost everyone in the tribe was washing sweet potatoes before eating them.

"The added energy of this hundredth monkey somehow created an ideological breakthrough!

"But notice.

"A most surprising thing observed by these scientists was that the habit of washing sweet potatoes then jumped over the sea –

"Colonies of monkeys on other islands and the mainland troop of monkeys at Takasakiyama began washing their sweet potatoes.

"Thus, when a certain critical number achieves an awareness, this new awareness may be communicated from mind to mind.

"Although the exact number may vary, this Hun-

85

dredth Monkey Phenomenon means that when only a limited number of people know of a new way, it may remain the conscious property of these people.

"But there is a point at which if only one more person tunes-in to a new awareness, a field is strengthened so that this awareness is picked up by almost everyone!"

Lyall Watson had originally researched and assembled the story from the available testimonies of the primate researchers. Because the phenomenon took the researchers so much by surprise, they had not counted how many monkeys it took to trigger this effect. So, Watson proposed an arbitrary figure of ninety-nine monkeys, and said that one more, the so-called one-hundredth monkey, would then provide the critical mass of consciousness necessary to trigger the effect.

The new behavior pattern spread to most, but not all, of the monkeys. Older monkeys, in particular, remained steadfast in their established behavior patterns and resisted change. When the new behavior pattern suddenly appeared among monkey troupes on other islands, only a few monkeys on those islands picked up on the new idea. The ones most receptive to new ideas started imitating the new behavior and demonstrating it to the impressionable younger ones. Thus, they too began their own path towards their eventual hundredth monkey effect.

The mechanism for this transference of ideas works the same way for monkeys as it does for all sentient beings. We exist within an atmosphere of global mind. The human brain is constantly receiving and transmitting mental pictures and information to and from that mental atmosphere in which we are immersed.

The global mind does not cease to function because a few skeptics don't like its effects. It functions just like it always has, passing information from one individual to another based upon their common frequency of consciousness. If progressive monkeys had a new idea, then so did other progressive monkeys on other islands. They resonated at the same frequency of consciousness.

Inventions often occur at the same time by inventors who are not in physical contact with each other. For example, in 1941, Les Paul designed and built the first solid-body electric guitar just when Leo Fender of Fender Musical Instruments was doing exactly the same thing.

Have you ever had an idea, then seen other people express, or use, that same idea? You probably said, "Hey! I thought of that first!" Well, that's the way the global mind works. It's an atmosphere that you share with all other sentient beings, but you tune in especially to the particular topics and frequencies of mind

87

that interest you the most.

The actual portion of a population required to reach the hundredth monkey effect is unknown, but it is a small portion. How is it possible that a small portion of the population can trigger a massive influence on the rest? What power do those people possess to have so much effect on society? And it's a silent influence, at that – a telepathic tidal wave that informs others about what's new. How could that possibly work?

Could it be that trend setters are operating at a slightly higher frequency of consciousness than the trend followers, and that the higher frequency carries with it a greater influence? That's exactly what David Hawkins discovered when he researched the scale of human consciousness.

You Are Changing The World

The book 'Power vs. Force: The Hidden Determinants in Human Behavior' by David Hawkins reveals some fascinating properties of human consciousness. In it, he created and calibrated an enormously useful map of human consciousness, one which should rightfully be called, 'The Hawkins Scale of Consciousness.'

Hawkins began practicing psychiatry in 1952, and then discovered the power of kinesiology, the science which obtains answers direct from the subconscious mind of a subject through muscle-testing.

The subconscious (or unconscious) mind is one segment of your total range of consciousness. The subconscious mind stores memories and emotional issues. It controls the involuntary nervous system, which manages such systems as breathing, digestion and metabolism. It is also in communication with the universe as a whole. In particular, it is connected to the global, or collective unconscious, mind of humanity.

The subconscious mind is, basically, the ultimate information source, one which is ready to provide information about anything upon demand.

With kinesiology, the subjects' conscious minds are bypassed in order to receive clear answers directly from their subconscious minds. The tests are mechanically very simple. Subjects hold out an arm horizontally to the side while people designated as testers tell the subjects to resist their efforts to push one arm down with each question. If the arm remains strong and stays horizontal, then the answer from the subconscious mind of the subject is affirmative. If the arm yields downwards due to weakness then the answer is negative.

If, for example, you tell a test subject to resist while you tell them, "You have a human body" their arm will stay strong. If you change the statement to, "You are a human body" their arm will go weak as this is an incorrect statement. The reason for this is that we, as spirits, merely inhabit our physical bodies. We are not our bodies, even though the ego tends to see us as who we are in the mirror. The subconscious mind knows that the true answer is, "You have a human body."

John Diamond, M.D., another early researcher in kinesiology, observed cases where the right and left hemispheres of a person's brain were working together. The left hemisphere of the brain is normally used for analytical thinking and verbal activity, while the right hemisphere is used for intuitive and artistic activities as well as spatial orientation.

90

This explains why it is so hard to drive a car at the same time as carrying on a telephone conversation. In order to pay attention to the road and the activities of other traffic, the driver has to switch from one hemisphere of the brain over to the other side, and then switch back again to continue the conversation.

In the rare cases where both hemispheres were working equally together, Diamond discovered that the person now displayed creativity, which he referred to as mankind's highest functioning.

David Hawkins found kinesiology to be a fascinating avenue into the unknown, and he began accessing what he calls attractor fields in the subconscious. Attractor fields are what Carl Jung called archetypes. They are created by the group efforts of millions of minds in the collective unconscious and hold a fascination for people because of their cumulative size.

Just when his practice became huge, with fifty therapists and other employees working for him, Hawkins abandoned it all for a life of research. Instead of treating one patient at a time, Hawkins wanted to discover how everyone could be helped by the promise and potential of kinesiology.

His research over the years proved conclusively

the same thing that the new theoretical physics is beginning to say, that everything in the universe is connected. With kinesiology, he confirmed that whatever question is asked, if there is an answer to that question somewhere in the universe, then that answer will become yours.

He also set up a system of calibrating levels of human consciousness. Assigning the numbers one to infinity as the possible range of consciousness, he soon found that he had to use the logarithm of numbers, rather than just plain numbers. This is because the power of consciousness at higher levels is vast compared to its power at lower levels.

When you use a base-ten logarithmic system, the number 4 is not twice the number 2. Log 4 is 10,000 (one plus four zeros) versus log 2's value of just 100 (one plus two zeros). A consciousness level of 300 is not twice 150, it is 10 to the 300th power; a one with 300 zeros after it.

Furthermore, Hawkins found that the consciousness level of 200 was critical. A global average of 200 or more is necessary to sustain life on this planet without it sinking into eventual self-destruction. Since the mid-1980s, he reports, the global average reading for humanity climbed above the critical 200 level. This, of course, is yet another discovery confirming the existence of today's ongoing shift in consciousness.

Then, he began to wonder how much people of higher consciousness were compensating for people who live below the 200 level. Consider, for example, that 800 million people in the world are hungry, with many of them living near starvation. The consciousness of despair tests at a level of just 50. Even anger and hatred rate higher in frequency than the deep depression experienced by those who live with no appearance of hope.

So here we are, on Planet Earth, a collective humanity swimming hard through life to keep our collective chins above the 200 level, working towards the day when hunger and hopelessness will be eradicated from our world once and for all.

What can you do to help? As you raise your consciousness, you contribute more and more to the spiritual quality of the global mind. Therefore, your greatest service to humanity is, paradoxically, the development of your own consciousness.

How exactly can that help the world? Getting back to modern science and its numbering systems, along with today's liking for summaries that spell out 'the bottom line,' here are the test results.

One individual at a higher level of consciousness counterbalances many, many individuals who are below the critical level of 200. Below the 200 level are the attractor fields of shame, guilt, apathy, grief, fear, desire, anger and pride. Right at the critical 200 level comes courage and its ability to empower the self out of the victim-orientation of the lower frequencies.

At 300, a person has risen above many emotions of conflict to achieve some non-judgment and to feel optimism. At 300, one person, within the global mind, counterbalances an incredible total of 90,000 people below the 200 level. Such is the power of higher states of consciousness.

At 400, the individual achieves a harmonious attitude which brings acceptance and forgiveness. Furthermore, they gain an enhanced sense of reason, which brings understanding and meaning to life. This is not a difficult level to achieve. Those who, for example, pursue higher education and the professions function at the 400 level, where one person counterbalances an incredible 400,000 people below the 200 level.

To reach 500, a person needs to be spiritually conscious. At this level, unconditional love and unconditional forgiveness become alive and well in their reality. Here, one person counterbalances 750,000 people who are below the 200 level.

When a person has practiced meditation long and diligently enough to attain bliss consciousness at the

600 level, they are, at that moment, counterbalancing 10 million people below the 200 level.

Do you need a more compelling reason to develop your inner faculties? Just look at the wonderful level of service that each advance in consciousness brings into our world.

And all this is by just being who you are and who you can become, before you even begin to physically help make the world a better place through your support and direct action. This wonderful level of service is the direct effect of your consciousness upon a world which has been starved, for so long, of spiritual thought and spiritual energy.

The Shift

Part III

What it Means to be Living in the New Reality

The Shift

Wholeness as the First Step into the New Reality

Meme number six is the preparatory stage towards New Reality consciousness. In this stage, people become heartfelt in their awareness. This passive phase of heart chakra awareness can manifest in many ways, one of which is environmental consciousness and community building.

Meme number seven is the active phase of heart chakra awareness. This is the first meme in the second tier of consciousness and the first and most important destination into The Shift. In this phase the person transforms from being heartfelt to being heart-powered.

In a shift from meme six to meme seven, people will transform from understanding through their heart to acting through their heart.

Instead of being, for example, alternative-lifestyle eco-enthusiasts building a sustainable home environment on a small scale, they are more likely to expand into thinking on a wider scale. They might say, "Hey, we can spread the eco-movement better if we produce this eco-friendly equipment - lots of it - and then go out and promote it to other people!"

If they support an organization that is helping make the world a better place, one that is special to them, they're more likely to decide to join the staff so that they can work there full-time.

The first manifestation of New Reality consciousness is a trend towards wholeness. Wholeness comes from the integration of mind, body and spirit into a synergistic harmony.

Inner wholeness is, basically, integrity without the 'shoulds.' Integrity, according to the dictionary, can mean wholeness, but it can also be interpreted in a way that carries a lot of baggage.

This add-on baggage includes self-defeating concepts like 'should,' 'try to,' and 'high' moral standards. All of these concepts are facets of Old Reality consciousness.

The frequency of consciousness in the New Reality is heart-centered. Unconditional love comes naturally; you need only let it flow through your heart and allow that energy to be who you are.

When you shift to the higher consciousness of the New Reality, the universe reorganizes itself around you to reflect that higher reality. Externally-imposed rules are replaced by internal, love-based choices.

To become whole is to become harmoniously fully functional. In such a reality, you treat yourself and others with unconditional love and care. To care less than that for yourself, or less than that for others, would mean being less than whole.

The keyword of the Old Reality was separation. The keyword for the New Reality is integration, as in a sense of wholeness. An integrated self does not have opposing parts which foster a loss of self-love and self-acceptance.

In the Old Reality, the Creator was seen as something outside of you, something separate from you. Physics today is proving that the universe is an interconnected whole, and that separation is an illusion, as are the concepts of time and space. If everything is one then you are not just connected to the Creator, you are an aspect of the Creator. That's the way the universe was designed. You are an aspect of the Creator with a unique viewpoint of the universe. Your role is to experience life from one of an infinite number of viewpoints. Your experience then contributes to the infinite whole, because all is one.

In the Old Reality, in order to maintain a sense of separation from the Creator, people were told:

a) That money was 'bad.' Money was the one

thing that provided independence in our society, and a sense of personal power made people less controllable by others and, in particular, those who claimed to represent the Creator.

b) That sex was 'bad.' This was particularly useful in controlling people. Something that is as natural as eating or sleeping is bound to keep vying for people's attention. So, if a natural inclination such as sex can be defined as bad, then permanent inner conflict can be guaranteed. Such a person becomes divided within themselves. As the Old Reality philosophy goes, in order to conquer you first have to divide. For example, Pope Innocent III (1160-1216 A.D.) even went so far as to say, "The sexual act is so shameful that it is intrinsically evil."

c) That intuition was especially 'bad.' After all, you couldn't have people acting on inner guidance when the aim was to keep them under external control. Women, being more intuitive than men, became natural targets for the power-hungry leaders of a growing, and growingly corrupt, movement which claimed to represent the Creator of all life. One of the darkest, fear-filled eras of history was created by redefining healers, herbalists, sensitives, and anyone who dared think for themselves, as witches who were in league with a convenient, pre-fabricated, imaginary enemy.

Well, so much for the Old Reality. It won't be missed. It was an intense and drama-filled stage of human experience, and now it is ending. The New Reality is dawning, and it brings new rules or, to be more precise, new principles. These new principles operate in the expanded vista of awareness that the New Reality brings.

In the New Reality, the frequency of consciousness is different. When you allow yourself to be in tune with this frequency, you no longer strive to be separate from others, nor do you strive to maintain opposing, separative points of view within yourself.

The New Reality is heart-centered and heart-powered

When you see fear for the hollow illusion that it is and allow your heart to open to everyone in your life, then your actions are determined by your unconditional love for others around you and, equally, for yourself. When your heart opens up to loving yourself as much as anyone else, then you do want the best for yourself, just as any parent wants the best for their child.

The Old Reality sees love of self as an egocentric problem. The New Reality recognizes that, if the original Creation includes infinite love, then perhaps it's time to get in tune with the greater reality and wholly respect yourself.

A heart-based reality is not an egocentric level of consciousness. It exists at a different frequency. Wholeness comes with a shift of focus from the faces of the solar plexus chakra to the heart chakra and the active channeling of heart-based, unconditional love.

With the shift to love energy comes wholeness of mind, body and spirit.

Twelve Principles for the New Reality

The New Reality brings with it a new vista of awareness. In order to operate successfully in the new environment, you need to apply the new principles which come with that expanded vision, that greater vista of reality.

Such knowledge empowers you to awaken to your newly expanded potential and to manifest that potential with ease.

When I was sixteen, my physics teacher said, "Basic principles, lad. When you know the basic principles, you can solve any problem." I have often thought how right he was. Here, we will examine some basic principles of the universe, as seen from the viewpoint, or the expanded vista, of the New Reality consciousness.

In this, the ultimate reality is recognized as universal consciousness, as the formative essence behind all that exists within the universe. I call that essence Infinite Being because it is the awareness behind everything within the universe. *Infinite*, as in All That Is. *Being*, as in fundamental awareness. Infinite Being is the deepest concept of God or The Ab-

105

solute.

Here are twelve principles which describe New Reality awareness.

1. Infinite Being is All That Is. Nothing exists outside of it.

The universe exists within the consciousness of Infinite Being. The physical world exists within the consciousness of Infinite Being. We exist within the consciousness of Infinite Being.

2. We are Infinite Being.

Creation is holographic in nature, meaning that the one can be found within the all. For example, the oak tree produces acorns and yet the life-form of a complete oak tree is contained within each acorn. If a picture hologram is divided into two, both parts will still retain the complete original picture.

While you are a part of the consciousness of Infinite Being, you are also Infinite Being itself. At the deepest level of reality, all that Infinite Being is, you are.

Therefore we are, each one of us, Infinite Being.

3. Purpose in life.

Your overall purpose in life is to experience it from one individual, unique point of view. Just as each snowflake is unique, so is each person. From a cosmic point of view, you are one expression of Infinite Being as it experiences itself from all possible viewpoints. In this way, through you and all life, Infinite Being gains infinite experience.

At a personal level, you, as a soul, pre-planned the major themes of your life. You chose the time, the place and your parents in order to set a life plan in motion which would explore those themes. Such pre-planning gave rise to the occurrence of related, meaningful events in your life which may have already given you the impression that destiny exists.

Destiny does exist, to the extent that the major themes of your life are pre-planned, by you, ahead of time.

As you pass through life, certain names, places, people and activities resonate with a certain specialness in your consciousness. It's almost as if you knew them once before, but you can't quite remember when or where. That is destiny, as it unfolds important, pre-planned and pre-viewed events into your life.

In the phenomenon called déjà vu, scenes that you recognize as they unfold in your life are scenes which you had previously viewed in another state of consciousness. This previewing occurred either during your pre-life planning or, more often, in a recent, out-of-body, dream-state where, in order to help yourself remain on-purpose, you reviewed the important, upcoming events in your life.

4. Free will enables you to explore your true potential.

Free will fills in all the details. It can be used to any degree that you choose. The most productive use of free will is to explore your true potential within the themes of your life, thus gaining the greatest possible experience from your life plan.

5. Reincarnation.

Reincarnation exists to provide a variety of experiences, so that life skills may be gained, and so that, while in a physical body, you can rediscover your spiritual connection within.

6. Life after 'death.'

From the point of view of your true, inner personality, passing away from the physical realm is like stepping out of a suit that you have worn for a while. The suit is not the real you. In your spirit body, you move into the spirit realm, which is a place of joy and healing. After meeting with friends and relatives who have passed on before, you start work on resolving the issues which caused inner conflict during your physical life. Then, as you move into the higher realms, remembering more about who you really are, you experience reunion with the rest of your immediate and extended soul families.

7. Life reflects what you project.

Reflectance is a property of the universe. Also known as karma, this principle states that life reflects your beliefs, emotions and actions. The stronger these are, the more apparent it becomes that life is a mirror of what you project.

Every time you change the way you view life, the universe, just like a mirror, reflects your new view of reality. This may not occur instantaneously as, often, circumstances do not allow the new reflection to immediately manifest. In this case, the new reality is held, like a pressure within the aura of your body's subtle magnetic field. You then walk around in life, surrounded by this magnetic potential, as it influences your circumstances to adapt into a form where the new reality will be able to manifest and operate.

Reflectance, sooner or later, produces manifestation. Therefore, if you don't like something in your life, the most powerful way to change its effect permanently is to discover how you are generating that reflection, and then change your point of view so that you change the reflection that you are causing from the universe.

That's how reflectance works. It's just like law in physics. It's how the universe was designed. The mirror of life will shine happiness upon you, but not until you first decide, within yourself, to become a happy person. Then it will reflect your new reality.

8. Abundance is natural.

Natural abundance comes from 'getting into the flow,' by doing work that brings a sense of inner excitement. The phrase "Follow your inner joy" is actually the key to abundance. Once you follow your innermost joy and adapt your situation to doing work that you love, then synchronicity begins to flow. Synchronicity is the universe's way of telling you that you're on the right track. It is a flow of events where everything starts clicking into place in order to support your efforts.

Synchronicity brings you opportunities, people, events and circumstances exactly when and where they need to be. When life flows naturally, the universe's natural state of abundance follows automatically.

9. Love is the only reality.

Unconditional, holistic love is the answer to all of life's challenges. We are here on Earth to learn how to love ourselves and others, and to accept ourselves and others completely, without judgment.

At this point, some people ask, "What, are you supposed to love someone who is bent on being anti-social, even destructive?" The secret here is that there is a difference between an acceptance of the outer beliefs of a person and an acceptance of their inner essence.

Regardless of that person's outward belief system, and whether you agree with it or not, it is the inner essence of the person that you learn to recognize, love and accept.

The secret is that unconditional love will heal the world, and there is no shortage of its supply. The universe is permeated by, and held together by, the love aspect of the one Creator. You have only to allow it to flow through you in order to experience its wonder.

10. Self-responsibility.

You create your own reality and take personal responsibility for it. Your life is a reflection of your point of view in this, the set of experiences that you, as a soul, planned for this life.

11. Truth is everywhere.

The ultimate truth is to be found within, yet the study of a variety of sources of information helps you to reawaken and remember your inner truth. Your intuitive sense is your guide as to what material is most appropriate for you at any particular time during your personal development.

12. Inner connection and insight.

Inner connection with your spiritual source promotes spiritual transformation and the achievement of your true potential. Developing intuition, both in men and women, provides an essential insight into life's experiences.

The way this is achieved is through regular, daily meditation. The regular practice of meditation promotes intuitive insight, unconditional love and personal spiritual experiences. Any meditation technique that you prefer will function perfectly well, but the Infinite Being meditation technique is particularly powerful.

With practice, you actually need no technique at all, because you will find that you can go into those deeper levels of awareness, whenever you wish, as an acquired habit. In the meantime, here is the ultimate door-opener to the higher realms of human consciousness, the Infinite Being meditation technique.

The Shift

The Ultimate Meditation

Peace can sometimes be so far away, and inner bliss… even farther away.

Take the time now to spend some real quality time by going within. Find that sense of peace that lies within. Visit the place where inner bliss dwells and waits patiently for your return.

Let yourself unwind and compose yourself for a few precious moments of peace. Remember that your mind is much more far-reaching than your physical brain. Your mind, as consciousness, is nonphysical, while your brain is just the physical translator of your consciousness.

Your mind, therefore, always has the ability to tell your brain;

"Shsh! It's meditation time!"

Focus your mind away from the clutter of day-to-day living and turn your attention towards the peaceful core of your inner being. Then think of the deepest possible state of consciousness.

And what could the deepest possible state of consciousness be?

It is the state of consciousness known as Infinite Being. The word Infinite reflects the idea of ultimate, while the word Being refers to a sense of awareness, rather than a doing activity. Infinite Being is infinite consciousness without a focus upon any specific action.

Infinite Being doesn't have to do anything, it already is everything.

It is important to appreciate that the state of Infinite Being is not 'out there' somewhere external to us. Infinite Being encompasses all consciousness, including all manifestation. We are that consciousness. We exist within it, as does everything else in existence.

The Infinite Being Meditation

In meditation practices, affirmations are often used to focus the mind. Simply by repeating the words "I am," you affirm your nature as consciousness. In the case of the Infinite Being meditation, we affirm our identity as the ultimate, infinite consciousness.

The affirmation "I am Infinite Being" is the most powerful affirmation possible within the English language.

The phrase "I am Infinite Being" is an affirmation of your oneness with the ultimate potential, the source of all life, the consciousness from which all life sprang. You are one with that universal consciousness. Everything in manifestation is one with that universal consciousness. Now is the time to consciously affirm your ultimate potential. It may take courage to begin with, but the results are more than worth the effort.

If you find issues arising, such as a feeling of unworthiness in your alignment with the 'All That Is,' with Infinite Being, just let those thoughts go, then gently bring your mind back into focus upon the phrase. You do not have to justify the words, or settle any internal argument about them, just because of some prior conditioning as to how someone said that you "should" think in this life.

Think independently, think infinitely, and you will connect with the consciousness of your ultimate potential.

Have the inner discipline to stay with the affirmation and let the issues fade away unchallenged. Your inner self knows the meaning of the words and resonates in joy with their exact and literal truth. Every time you make this affirmation, you become more connected with Infinite Being. Any lesser thoughts are then healed within the light of greater truth.

Find a quiet space to sit down for a few minutes, close your eyes, and start looking for that quiet space within. To keep your brain occupied with the task at hand, focus your attention on the slow, even flow of breath as it passes in and out of your nostrils.

As you breathe each in-breath, mentally repeat the affirmation "I am Infinite Being."

On the out-breath, simply allow your attention to follow the flow of air from your nostrils. To induce an immediate calming effect, allow each out-breath to take longer than each in-breath.

Life energy, also known as etheric energy, is conditioned primarily within the etheric counterpart of the spinal column. From there it is distributed to the rest of the body via the subtle nervous system. Most key functions in the human body owe their operation primarily to the supply of etheric life energy, rather than to the supply of electrical energy. Etheric energy, like consciousness, is non-physical and yet is behind all life.

To help enhance the natural flow of life energy within your spine when you perform this meditation it is preferable to sit with your spine straight. As you progress with this meditation, the natural flow of life energy will increasingly bring an enlivened awareness to your consciousness.

When distracting thoughts arise - which they will - treat them with patience and understanding. Put each distracting thought aside so that you can continue with the Infinite Being meditation. If a thought seems important or urgent, then it will be sure to return later, after your meditation session has finished.

There are a number of ways to enhance your meditation experience. One is to reserve a small space, such as the corner of a quiet room, where only meditation is conducted. That space then becomes more conducive to a meditation environment. A small table or surface can be covered with items that you connect with spiritual practice. Candles and incense are especially useful as they provide some initial focus for the senses.

It also helps to always use the same chair, one that is constructed primarily of a non-metallic material. Metal chairs attract etheric life energy away from you, which is great for the chair, but not so good for the meditation session.

A small clock completes your setting, so that you can take a peek if you have to finish on time. Clean, light clothing, reserved especially for meditation, further enhances the atmosphere. A shower or bath before meditation is very valuable. If, for example, you have just come home from a hectic day at work, then your energy body will be filled with the distractions of the day in etheric energy form.

The water that cleanses you in a shower or bath not only cleanses you of physical impurities, but, more importantly, it also cleanses the etheric energy impurities that do not belong in your energy body.

The reason that water is such an effective energy cleanser lies in its chemical composition. Water consists of H_2O - hydrogen and oxygen. Oxygen is not just a chemical that the body needs. Its greater role is to carry life-giving, etheric energy. When you shower, your etheric body is being washed with the water's flow of cleansing, etheric energy.

Make the Time for This to Happen

The best investment of your time each day is to spend 20 minutes in meditation. Make the time for this to happen. Make it the day's first priority. The easiest habit to adopt is one which makes meditation the first activity of the day. Making it a routine will also reinforce the effects of the meditation.

If you are hungry to the point of distraction before a meditation session, then have some light refreshment, such as fruit or juice. Conversely, a full stomach after a heavy meal will have a deadening effect upon the higher possibilities of your meditation session, so plan to eat any large meals at least two hours before your session, or wait until after the session.

The Aims of the Infinite Being Meditation

a) To quiet your daily brain activity by focusing on rhythmic activities that induce a spiritual focus.

b) To affirm your connection to the highest possible state of awareness.

c) To charge your system with additional life energy through controlled breathing.

The Infinite Being Meditation Technique in Summary

1) Focus your attention on the slow, even flow of breath as it passes in and out of your nostrils.

2) As you breathe each in-breath, mentally repeat the affirmation "I am Infinite Being."

3) On the out-breath, allow your attention to follow the flow of air from your nostrils. To induce an immediate calming effect, slow each out-breath and allow it to take up to twice as long as each in-breath. Feel the body relaxing as you breathe out.

4) Repeat this cycle of breathing for 20 minutes.

Remember

The affirmation "I am Infinite Being" is the most powerful affirmation possible within the English language.

Happy surfing upon the realms of spiritual awareness!

How You as a Soul Planned Your Life

Your inner self, your soul, remembers your life plan perfectly, even though your conscious mind does not. Fortunately, your conscious mind is not left to wander by itself, rudderless and adrift, in a world of free will.

One of the functions of your inner self is to give you hunches that your conscious mind can follow. These hunches, which can be very subtle and yet still effective, assist you to explore your life's potential to the fullest effect.

Your inner self, besides being your connection with the ultimate state of Infinite Being, is also your primary personal guide in life. Often, people also have one or two spirit guides. These are normally other members of their soul family who occasionally visit when they sense that they are needed to offer helpful, spiritual advice in the form of hunches.

Your primary guide is still your inner self, so, remember, when it comes to making difficult decisions, nobody knows you like your inner self does.

Your inner self could also be called your complete self, because it incorporates all aspects of your mind. Your whole consciousness includes your waking-state, conscious mind, and also the subconscious and superconscious aspects of your mind.

Regular, daily meditation keeps you in tune with your inner self and helps to guarantee that you get the most out of life by being in the right places at the right times. Then, synchronicity begins to unfold in the form of meetings and events which support your life's purpose.

Your soul is a member of an extended family consisting of many hundreds of other souls. All of these people have known and loved you for thousands of years, so, when you are planning a new life, there are always ample opportunities to be born through parents that you already know at a soul level. Usually, people choose lives where they can surround themselves with members of their extended soul family because people in the same soul family share common themes. They are in tune with your consciousness and, therefore, are interested in the same issues and experiences in life.

Before the Veil of Birth

When it was time for you to incarnate into this life, you viewed several alternatives, including several possible sets of parents. Your final choice offered you the best opportunity to explore the activities and issues that you have been experiencing.

How much detail goes into planning an entire lifetime? Destiny exists for the main events in your life – the major choices, events and connections in your life. Important relationships are carefully planned so that they have the best chance of happening. Your parents and your environment are chosen for how they will mold your life in the direction that you wish to explore.

In the pre-life planning stage, you actually get to see how everything will turn out as you explore different alternatives and scenarios. Then you make your big choice. You say, "I'll take Fred and Freda Smith as parents. I'll be their baby boy, starting in nine months when I get born. Until then I'll hang around them in spirit, at least on and off, until it's time to emerge and become a baby person.

"Then I'll grow up in their family, attending that local elementary school. When they move to Phoenix as planned, I'll go to high school there and meet my old buddy, who'll be called Freddie, and he'll be the same age as me. Sylvia's family will move into town when I'm sixteen, and my being her boyfriend will start to shape the direction of the rest of my life. We'll go to the same college together and explore the idea that I can support her while she goes on to medical school to become a doctor, because that's how her life plan will be running at that point in time."

And so on, and so on, as the plan unfolds.

It becomes like a stage play with many players, all interacting at crucial points. Later, as the drama unfolds during your actual lifetime, your soul gets busy inspiring you to make sure that you'll be at the right place at the right time for each of those critical points.

Themes, Issues, Adventures

Your life plan will include personal themes and sometimes themes that your soul family wishes to pursue. Also, there are cultural themes and global issues, especially with today's growing global awareness. One theme that society has been developing over the last few decades is the issue of recovering from the imbalance of a patriarchal society.

At the same time, an even larger shift has been taking place – the shift from a consciousness of separation to one of integration. Separation consciousness has been the theme for thousands of years. We have separated into tribes, then countries and empires. We have separated ourselves by race, sex and religion. We have even separated our own consciousness, focusing it further into the external world and away from the inner light which is the very source of our consciousness.

One of the first differences that will be noticed as the world evolves towards integrated consciousness is that people will care more about their work. Most people today see their work as a means to an end, as a way to pay the bills and maybe get ahead a little.

Tomorrow, people will work at what they love and they will care deeply about the quality of service that they provide, because they will care for their customers. Of course, there are people who work just like that today, but they are in the minority. Tomorrow, it will become the new standard, the new work ethic. Loving what you do and doing what you love.

Basically, even when you're knee-deep in issues, remember that the purpose of life is to transform reality and to have fun doing it.

The Shift

128

What is Real?

What is real? What is there to hold on to?

One of the main reasons for experiencing life on Earth is to discover what is real.

We spend our lives coming here, going there, trying this and trying that. We acquire physical things and eventually let them go. Life's experiences pass by like so much water under the bridge.

One constant in all of life's ever-changing realities is the inner observer. This aspect of your inner self is present in all of life's experiences, watching, learning, remembering. However, when you go even deeper than this, you reach the underlying basis of all consciousness, the awareness that, simply, you exist.

This fundamental awareness can be summarized in two words: "I am."

The All-Pervasive, "I Am" Presence

You are one individual viewpoint of the great I Am, the consciousness of All That Is, the all-inclusive and all-embracing Infinite Being.

129

Consciousness is reality. Experiences may change from minute to minute, but underneath the flow of experiences lies that constant awareness, the sense of being that says, "I am."

Life is about experiences which unfold at different locations in space and time.

A universe in motion makes possible the changes we call experience. But if life is constantly changing, then what is there to hold on to? What is unchangingly real?

Infinite Being is the underlying reality. Infinite Being is all that is, it never changes. This state of *being* is pure awareness, pure potential, whereas *doing* is the acting out of that potential.

The underlying reality of Infinite Being is complete beingness. Infinite Being is real. It never changes. It always is; just is.

How do you connect with reality? By meditating, by using the affirmation, "I am Infinite Being," you can build your connection daily to the true reality which lies within you.

When you practice meditation at the start of each day, then daily meditation becomes a habit, something which occurs with ease. By building that inner bridge to reality, you are empowering your own potential and also helping to shift the global mind towards the enlightenment of the New Reality.

The Shift

Being as Well as Doing

Many Core Cultural Creatives have a nagging doubt about life, one which comes and goes and sometimes troubles them deeply. They intuitively feel that they are here on Earth to help humanity, but they just can't seem to figure out what exactly they are supposed to be doing about it.

The problem really comes from our current training in Western society. We are taught, from a very early age, to do things and achieve outward results, to build monuments of our outward 'doingness' for all to see.

But, what about 'beingness?'

The answer to the dilemma lies in understanding that there is a difference between doing and being, and your state of being does make a difference. It actually affects the mass consciousness of the world. The research behind the Hawkins Scale of Consciousness reveals the enormous power of just being, especially when you raise your consciousness in order to be the best you can be. You can support literally millions of people on planet Earth just by virtue of who you are, by being a person conscious at one of the higher memes or chakras.

Remember, to reach 500 on the Hawkins Scale of Consciousness, a person needs to be spiritually conscious. At this level, unconditional love and unconditional forgiveness become alive and well in their reality. Here, one person counterbalances 750,000 people who are below the 200 level.

When a person has practiced meditation long and diligently enough to attain bliss consciousness at the 600 level, they are, at that moment, counterbalancing 10 million people below the 200 level.

Your chakra system is designed to receive energy from the cosmos and from the local environment. Your thoughts and feelings condition life energy as it passes through you, out into the mental environment, or the atmosphere of the global mind. The chakras are receiving and transmitting devices for mental and life energy. An individual is like a radio station - you transmit whatever program you are playing internally.

When you are operating from the frequencies of your upper chakras, the second tier of memes, you are operating in spiritual service to the world. The second tier is spiritual in nature. When your awareness is functioning in the second tier, you are spiritually conditioning the atmosphere of the global mind and making the world a better place.

While you are here on Earth, you are contributing who you are – your thoughts, your dreams and your passion for life – into the atmosphere of a global mind that is hungry for, more than anything else, spiritual light.

The Shift

Your Nine-Point New Reality Plan

To step forward into New Reality consciousness means to experience new vistas of awareness and new levels of creativity. It means following your heart to express your inner joy through making your own meaningful contribution towards the betterment of the world.

Inner joy and fulfillment are your natural birth-rights. It takes a New Reality-style focus to develop and enhance your sense of inner joy. Then, the term 'quality of life' takes on an entirely new dimension, one which expands along with the widening vistas of your new awareness.

The Nine-Point New Reality Plan employs the most powerful formula in the universe. It is the same formula that the original consciousness of Infinite Being used to make the creation of the universe possible.

When Infinite Being created the universe, it had no other tools but consciousness at its disposal, so the Creation was initiated by just three aspects of consciousness.

137

1. Thought

2. Feeling

3. Action

Infinite Being used its imagination, or its faculty of thought, like an architect. Then, expressing its feeling as the love which, even today, fills the universe and holds it together, Infinite Being set the whole symphony of Creation into motion. Everything in the universe today has been formed from that original formula of 'Thought and Feeling in Action.'

Thought, in this formula of creation, refers to intellect, and feeling is listed as a separate function. In practice, people's thoughts and feelings are intertwined, and they are experienced only when they are set into motion. The three express as the one. Thought and feeling in action work together to produce the experiences within our lives. If you want to create a better reality in your life, this is the exact formula to use for the best results.

The phenomenon of a triad, or three elements acting as one, is very common in Nature. Light, for example, is electromagnetism, vibrating at a certain frequency. It has an electric component and a magnetic component, but the two are intertwined as electromagnetism, and then set into motion in order to manifest light. Light is the expression of all three components of a triad, acting together as one.

The Nine-Point New Reality Plan consists of three main groups, each of which is based upon the elements of the original Creation formula of thought, feeling and action. Then, to amplify its effectiveness even further, each group contains its own triad within it.

When you have three triads making up one main triad, you not only have the power of Creation working for you, you have it working for you multiplied – raised to the power of three, in fact. Do feel free to expect, and receive, miracles from this plan, as the potential for miracles is designed into the system.

In the first group of three, matters related to thought and intellect are addressed. Then, in the second group, matters of the heart – feeling – are brought into play and, finally, the whole plan is manifested through the third group, where inspired action is carried out in the physical world.

Use the Nine-Point New Reality Plan as a framework for contacting and expressing the powerful creativity which resides within you.

Your Nine-Point New Reality Plan

Overview

Here is an overview of the structure of this triad of triads which makes up the Nine-Point New Reality Plan.

1. Thought.

Learning. The expansion of your knowledge.

Health awareness and education to preserve your potential for fulfillment in life.

Skills development. The ability to express your learning.

2. Feeling.

Inner connection as a conscious decision, an awareness of your spiritual nature.

Meditation practice to develop this inner connection.

Experiencing the inner joy that you discover as you develop spiritually.

3. Action.

Applying creativity to your work as an expression of your knowledge.

Practice gratitude for everything in your life.

Service: Helping others through work that expresses your inner joy.

Detailed Descriptions

LEARNING

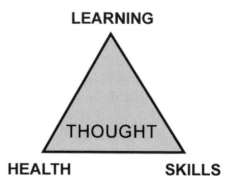

HEALTH   **SKILLS**

First: The Triad of Thought provides the resources for self-empowerment.

1. Learning

New knowledge can be acquired by attending various learning institutions, but it is self-directed education which opens the door to endless possibilities.

At school I was educated by others. At college I was educated by others. Once I had left college, I discovered self-education. There is no comparison between the two. Instead of wading through someone else's curriculum, with self-education you read whichever book is the most intriguing for you at the time. Self-education is not just an avenue of endless discovery, it is also an act of self-empowerment.

Self-education is something that you owe to yourself as a free spirit upon planet Earth. Study what you love and love what you study.

Personally, my favorite subject has always been what I call Holistic Metaphysics, which is the study of the nature of the universe and beingness, including the spiritual dimension. This addresses the whole mind-body-spirit spectrum along with such issues as why humans have potential, and what fun it can be to learn how to express that potential.

2. Health

Health education and awareness empowers you to live an active life, one which can be free from the limitations of the ill health caused by many of today's lifestyles.

Alternative health care is a massive field which is currently coming into its own. Self-education in this field is vital. When you study your options for health care, use your intuition to home in on the methods that are best for you. If your sense of intuition isn't functioning clearly, then practice regular, daily meditation until it does serve your decision-making process.

To enjoy life, you need good health. The big challenge today is that we live in a toxic world. The air, the water, and the ground are all loaded with a profusion of harsh chemicals, with toxicity that challenges the immune systems of everyone.

Good health is no mystery. If your level of toxicity reaches overload, your resistance fails and you fall victim to a variety of degenerative diseases. Drugs – the public's desire for a quick fix – usually just mask the symptoms, and add more toxicity to your delicate body systems. So, what can you do to reduce toxicity and get on the right track for better health?

First, eat organic foods. Organic fruits and vegetables are free of deadly, bug-killing chemicals. If pesticides are designed to kill via poisoning, then how much good can they be for your health when you eat their residue? Also, organic food does not have its shelf life extended by irradiating it into a dead-state using nuclear waste.

Health food enthusiasts have long promoted the virtues of a vegetarian diet. Some go even further and live on a vegan diet, which is free from eggs and dairy products. Avoiding the low vibratory frequency of meats is an obvious, intuitive move for people with certain health challenges. However, glowing health has not always resulted from such well-intentioned dietary restrictions. For example, a vegan diet can include such items as pasta, bread and boxes of processed crackers, which contain little or no life-giving, etheric energy.

What does work well, people are now beginning to realize, is the addition of living foods into the diet. Living foods are raw, uncooked fruits, vegetables, nuts and seeds. They are filled with their original life force and they include their own digestive enzymes, which are ready to serve your body's energy level and good health.

The secret of enzymes is that every food contains the enzymes required for its digestion. That's how the food cycle in Nature was designed. Now, cooking destroys those in-built enzymes, forcing your body to try to make up for them from its own resources. So when you think 'raw,' think 'easy to digest.' That means that your body can spend its energy on improving your health, instead of fighting an uphill battle to handle the digestion of cooked food, which is not only enzyme-dead, but loses natural life energy during cooking.

When you think about it, the design specifications for the human body are that your body will gain nutrition from fruits, vegetables, nuts and seeds. Think 'Garden of Eden' here, as in, "Psst! Want an apple?" The original design spec for the human diet did not include the word 'cooked.' Cooking is a human invention.

You can avail yourself of the powerful health

benefits of living foods. Basically, the more raw fruits and vegetables that you include in your diet, the more your body will thank you for it.

Think about fresh fruits and fresh juice in the morning for breakfast and then, again, for a mid-morning snack. Great snack items for mid-afternoon include carrots with celery or almonds with raisins.

For dinner and/or lunch, mixed greens and raw veggies make a big, mixed, dinner salad, which you can toss in an olive oil-based dressing.

The secret of success is to always fill up on the healthy stuff first, then you don't find your self overdoing anything that you really didn't want to overdo.

Living foods – the foods that our bodies are designed to eat – have great potential for restoring our natural state of vibrant health.

3. Skills

The more skills you develop, the more you enjoy life. Often, the most enjoyable kind of work is creative work, and it requires creative skills. The good news is that creative skills are fun to learn as well as practice.

Self-training is the most convenient way to ac-

quire skills. If you need a teacher and/or some support from others on the same path, then community
colleges can offer the best value, while commercial
courses usually produce fast results.

The gaining of new skills causes a great chain
reaction. The more skills you have, the more valuable
you are to others, so the more you earn and the less
you have to worry about mundane financial matters.
Or, if you don't particularly need more income but
you love doing a certain kind of unpaid charitable
work, then you can work less and be free to spend
more time with your charitable work.

Second: The Triad of Feeling

CONNECTION

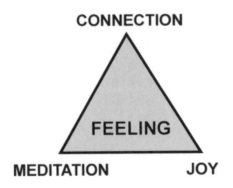

MEDITATION   JOY

This is where you discover your inner resources.

1. Connection

You connect with your inner self, first, by becoming consciously aware of that presence within you. Be aware that there are different frequencies for the different realms of consciousness.

Old Reality consciousness vibrates at the level of the intellectual (solar plexus) chakras. New Reality consciousness vibrates at the level of the holistic-active (heart) chakra. Your inner self, or soul, exists at the level of the creative (throat) chakras. This makes your heart the doorway to inner guidance from your inner self. It is in the silence of subtle intuition that impressions float gently into your awareness.

Be receptive to intuitive hunches. Train yourself to stop and consider what it means when an unexpected impression floats into your awareness. When it happens three times in a row, you're being given guidance which is persistent because of its importance.

2. Meditation

People practice meditation to achieve deeper states of consciousness. First, however, they often find that emotional blockages arise so that they can be healed and released. Emotional blockages are defensive reactions to past trauma. They exist to protect you from being hurt again, but they can also block your adventures into higher awareness. This is why they come to the surface for attention.

When you meditate, you can make a point of asking your inner self what blockages may be in the way of your further progress. Ask your inner self for guidance as to what is appropriate to release next. Your inner self knows of any and all issues that you might be ready to deal with, and it knows exactly when you are ready to dissolve and move through each one.

Your inner self uses the language of symbols. It can also speak English, and probably many other languages perfectly well, but the easiest way for your inner self to communicate with your conscious awareness during meditation is through the language of symbols.

When you are working through emotional issues in dreams, for example, notice how a dream often makes no logical sense, but the symbols in it represent your emotions and issues. In dream analysis, if you discard logic and just ask what each symbol means to you emotionally, then a dream can suddenly make a lot of sense. Dreams are often a kind of an echo chamber where you reflect upon, and work through, issues which have recently concerned you.

In meditation, you can use your conscious awareness to directly focus upon issues which need working through. When you have time for a meditation longer than the usual twenty minutes, take the time to ask your inner self to show you symbols that represent the issues that you next need to address. If you need help in finding solutions to those issues, then ask for the solutions to enter your consciousness.

3. Joy

The result of your conscious connection and regular meditation practice is that you find and experience inner joy.

Inner joy is waiting, right inside you, to bathe your consciousness in its constant supply of love and gentle upliftment. This is not imagination or wishful thinking, it is down-to-earth, holistic metaphysics. Inner joy resonates at the holistic (heart) chakra levels of consciousness. Once you get into a deeper state of meditation, you're right there, vibrating at the inner joy level of consciousness. You can't miss it! Anyone who says it isn't there, hasn't been there.

Once you dissolve any inner blocks and reach heart-powered consciousness, you will never want to look back. After all, how could you, when inner joy makes life so much fun?

Third: The Triad of Action

CREATIVITY

ACTION

GRATITUDE   SERVICE

You can manifest your joy though action in the following ways.

1. Creativity

Now that you have all that new knowledge and skills from the thought triad, here comes the fun part. You get to practice those skills as creativity in your work and in your hobbies.

In your work, applying creativity means finding and applying new solutions to new situations in order to better serve your customers. The more you learn, the more you are able to achieve an overview of each situation and innovate accordingly.

With creative hobbies, such as music, it used to be that music was created for a band or an orchestra to play. Now, with some technical skills as well as your music skills, you can perform on all the instruments in the band, then add your vocals and multi-track everything together. Who needs to play just bass guitar when you can play everything, and sing both the lead and accompaniment parts as well?

It used to be that an artist had to mix their paints and sit in front of a canvas in order to develop and express their talent. Today, computer software comes to the aid of the aspiring artist and makes expressions of art possible that were unheard of in the days of manual painting. Watch out, Michelangelo, a whole new generation of artistic creatives are launching themselves into a world which is ready for new talent, amplified by technology.

2. Gratitude

Giving thanks is the expression of gratitude, and having a grateful heart is one of the most beautiful secrets of spiritual life. Take the time to practice feeling gratitude for everything in your life.

Gratitude is a form of love, and love is something which flows from the Creator of the universe through all forms of life and manifestation. Without love, life in the universe cannot exist. Love is the universal force of preservation which holds creation in manifestation.

When you allow your heart to open to the universe's flow of love, gratitude comes with that flow. Gratitude for being alive, for just existing, for just being in the flow of the adventure of life. Gratitude for everything that you have. Gratitude for the Sun that gives us life. Gratitude for the Earth that gives us our home in the cosmos. Gratitude for the people that you love, and for those who share your journey through life.

Gratitude flows unimpeded from an open heart. When you allow it, it flows as freely as the sunshine, unobstructed by judgments or conditions.

One of the most endearing things a person can say to a loved one is this:

"I'm grateful for having you in my life, and I appreciate you for who you are."

Express gratitude for good service that you receive from people who perform work for you. If they respond in like mind, they are likely to provide even better service for you in the future.

3. Service

Service to others is a concept also known as right action. Right action is that which springs from within, from your spiritual heart or your inner self.

In the Old Reality, devoting your life in service to others often meant becoming a monk or a nun, taking vows of poverty, and then hoping that you didn't have second thoughts later in life.

In the New Reality, a self-empowered sense of individual purpose comes with the package. There are no pre-packaged, one-size-fits-all paths to enlightenment. These days, you have to determine your own avenue of service to humanity, based upon how your inner joy best needs to express itself.

In the New Reality, people realize that the way they serve humanity the best is by doing work that they love the most. This applies to both paid occupations and to charitable volunteer work. If you love what you do, you will do it so much better than you would if you were just going through the motions, without your heart being involved with your actions.

Doing what you love leads to expanding opportunities to serve people even better than before. This is because, in time, you become naturally adept at work that you love enough to become absorbed by it.

When you are doing work that you love, then time passes quickly. If long hours are needed, you do the extra work without feeling any emotional strain. You attend to all the fine details of your job because that's the work you like to do. Because of this, you soon become highly competent in your work.

At that point, progress happens in ways which amplify your ability to meaningfully serve others. Employed people are often promoted within their organization or promoted through being discovered by other employers. Self-employed people find their customer base expanding rapidly as word gets around that they are very good at their work.

When you follow your heart, you express your inner joy through meaningful service to humanity. You are using your talents to benefit others in your own unique way.

Remember, every creative genius in history was a person pursuing the activity that they loved the most. Composers like Mozart and Beethoven, artists like Rembrandt and Monet, scientists like Einstein and Galileo are all icons of dedicated creativity. They were all totally absorbed in work that they loved.

Let service to others through work that you love become your greatest inspiration, and let it produce your greatest accomplishments in life.

The Shift

It's a Great Time To Be Alive!

The Shift is the mass migration of humanity into the second tier of consciousness. This is where basic values transform into spiritual values, where caring hearts blossom forth into action to serve humanity in ways that represent their personal, highest joy.

Millions of pioneering trail-blazers have already made it through The Shift and into the new awareness. Every day, more people follow their example. The New Reality presents a newly emerging type of humanity. This vanguard of unconditional love and renewed hope holds the seeds of a culture where 'quality of life' replaces 'standard of living' and 'you-and-me' cooperation replaces 'you-versus-me' competition.

The world is transforming; destiny is calling. Together we are witnessing the dawning of the New Reality as it rises in all of its glory, like the Sun rising at the dawn of a bright, new day.

The New Reality is both heartfelt and heart-powered. It's about people who care. But people can only awaken to their new, expanded potential when they realize that this potential exists.

157

Tell your friends that the world is shifting to a new reality and that it is destined to become a truly beautiful place.

To step forward into New Reality consciousness means to experience new vistas of awareness and new levels of creativity. It means following your heart to express your inner joy through making your own meaningful contribution towards the betterment of the world.

It truly is a great time to be alive!

About the Author

Owen Waters is an international spiritual teacher who has presented his insights into the New Reality to hundreds of thousands of seekers. In 1963, at the age of just thirteen, he encountered his first spiritual awakening. The surprise of this mystical experience was such that his life became focused upon a continuous search for spiritual answers.

Almost forty years of study and research followed, along with the development of his inner vision. By the year 2002, like many of the spiritual teachers who are coming forward to help with today's shift in consciousness, his realizations began to unfold rapidly.

Today, as Editor and cofounder of Infinite Being Publishing LLC, he promotes a philosophy of spiritual empowerment through inner connection to the source of ultimate human potential.

People say that his material on the Infinite Being web site is warm, helpful, insightful, enlightening, profound, and yet easy to understand. Some say that reading his material is like remembering something they had forgotten long ago.

Owen writes a free newsletter at www.InfiniteBeing.com, where you can sign up to receive his regular articles on how to enjoy life to fullest in today's New Reality. Also, www.InfiniteBeing.com, you can view a selection articles and special reports, such as "The Seven K Secrets to Creating a Better Reality."